I0086961

I AM
Creating My
Own Dreams

by
Barry Thomas Bechta

**UNCONDITIONAL
LOVE BOOKS**

*Redefining, Guiding, and Inspiring Humanity's
Connection to the Creative Power within.*

I AM Creating My Own Dreams
by
Barry Thomas Bechta

© 2009 by BARRY THOMAS BECHTA

All rights reserved. No part of this book may be reproduced or transmitted in any form or by any means, electronic or mechanical, including photocopying, recording, or any information storage and retrieval system without written permission from the author, except for the inclusion of brief quotations in a review.

Library and Archives Canada Cataloguing in Publication

Bechta, Barry Thomas, 1968-
   I am creating my own dreams / by Barry Thomas Bechta.

ISBN 978-0-9686835-2-1

   1. Self-realization--Religious aspects.
2. Spiritual life. I. Title.

BL624.B434 2009   204   C2009-905852-9

Publisher's Note

This publication is designed to provide accurate and authoritative information in regard to the subject matter covered. It is sold with the understanding that the author/publisher is not engaged in rendering psychological, legal, or other professional service. If advice or other assistance is required in those areas, the services of a competent professional should be sought.

I AM
Creating My
Own Dreams

This
book is dedicated
to the Mind of God.
There are no unrealistic Dreams
in the Mind of God. There are only
unrealistic time lines in the mind of man.

ACKNOWLEDGMENTS

Once I fully started to acknowledge God's Presence in my life, my life fully started. Thank You God for this truth.

I AM grateful to Binah C Godisall for the love we share together. I AM Grateful that our Dreams Uplift and Encourage our Shared Joy of Love, Life, and God.

Thank You Anthony and Zachary. You have helped me grow and open my heart in ways that were inconceivable before you were there.

Loving thanks to Stephen, Margaret, Gabe, and Sam. Your laughter and love continues to bless my life.

Warm thanks to my family by blood and by love. I AM so grateful that my Loving family grows in feeling each day.

I AM extremely grateful to all the authors that continually inspire me to challenge and expand any limits in my view of God, Love, and Life. The works of these Authors and Creators: Iyanla Vanzant, Esther and Jerry Hicks with ABRAHAM, Louise L. Hay, Neale Donald Walsch, Eckhart Tolle, Dr. Wayne W. Dyer, Marianne Williamson, Jamie Sams, Dr. Norma J. Milanovich, Robert T. Kiyosaki, Alan Cohen, Mark Victor Hansen, John Randolph Price, Terry Cole-Whittaker, Richard Bach, Michael J. Losier, Richard Paul Evans, Sandra Ponder, Robert G. Allen, Og Mandino, Shakti Gawain, Prince, Marc Allen, Lenedra J. Carroll, Anthony Robbins, Deepak Chopra, Paul Ferrini, Faye Mandell, Brock Tully, Helen Schucman & William Thetford, Gary Zukav, Herman Hesse, Joe Vitale, Jack Canfield, Tom Johnson, Barbara Sher, Pat O'Bryan,

Once again thank you to everyone who has ever helped me in any way over the years.

And Most Importantly You, reading this right now.

I love all of you very much.

TO THE READER

If Dreams were easy everyone would have them easily.

If Dreams were simple everyone would have them simply.

If Dreams were effortless everyone would have them effortlessly.

If Dreams were what everyone believed and intended everyone would have what everyone believed and intended. In fact, this is exactly what everyone Creates - we always Create our deepest heartfelt most secret Beliefs and Intentions.

My Dreams have always come true. More to the point my deepest heartfelt Beliefs and Intentions have always come true. My Beliefs and Intentions are not the same as my Dreams. My Beliefs and Intentions are who and what I believe at the very deepest levels. My Dreams are who and what I wish I were. Until I Create Consciously, my deepest Beliefs and Intentions are rarely congruent with my Dreams.

I wrote *I AM Creating My Own Dreams* as my personal Blessing Bible; a tool to immediately connect with the Blessings available in my life. My blessings powerfully bless my life when I AM Being Enthusiasm and Being Open.

Being Enthusiasm occurs when I release my attachments to my past emotions and to my future expectations. I release my attachments when I can accept everything in my life that I previously found as unacceptable. When I have difficulty releasing my attachments or accepting what is currently in my life, it is rarely possible for me to truly Be Enthusiasm. When I AM caught up in past pains, present problems, or future fears, I Create mediocre Dreams since God's Abundant, Loving, and Successful Nature Manifests through me only the Dreams I Imagine in my mind.

The Process of Being Open involves accepting the possibility that my Dreams are already complete in the Mind of God. Particularly all my Dreams that I believe society may think are inappropriate, my family would never approve of, and of course the Dreams that seem blasphemous in their intent. The only one believing those truths about my Dreams is me - until I no longer choose to believe and intend those very things. Being Open is the process of Being Open to Change my limiting beliefs and intentions that deny my Dreams into Beliefs and Intentions that

Consciously Create them.

I AM Creating My Own Dreams when I AM Enthusiasm through my deepest held Dreams and I AM Open to Change in order to Create my personal Dreams. The only thing that ever needs to Change is my Beliefs and Intentions. I Consciously Choose to Create my Dreams.

I know you are Consciously Choosing to Create yours too.

Beautiful Blessings
Barry Thomas Bechta

TABLE OF CONTENTS

Every being communicates with God using their Heart, Mind, and Being.

God communicates with every being within their Heart, Mind, and Being.

I AM FIRE

The Feeling of God is the Fire I AM. God is the All That Is. God is the One That Is. There is Only God. God is the Only Activity, the Only Thought, the Only Spirit, and the Only Being I AM. God is constantly being God.

I AM a part of God's Oneness. God constantly expresses through me. I AM constantly Choosing what God expresses through me. I Choose what God is through my thoughts, feelings, words, and actions. Whatever I think, feel, say, and do is manifested by God when I Believe it with all my Heart, Mind, and Being. God always in all ways manifests at the level of my deepest Beliefs.

God is Unconditional Love. God's Energy is impersonal. God's Energy is constant. God's Energy is naturally Abundant, Successful, and Loving. It comes to every being in experience in the exact same Abundant, Successful, and Loving form. The only thing that is different for each being in God/Life/Energy is their individual thoughts, feelings, words, and actions.

Every being communicates with God using their Heart, Mind, and Being. God communicates with every being within their Heart, Mind, and Being. God is the voice Giving Ongoing Direction to every being in experience. God is All That Is. God's Energy flows to every being constantly, and Manifests whatever each being holds in their heart, mind, and being.

Since God's Energy is Unconditional, it always Creates outer experiences that match my deepest heartfelt most secret beliefs. God/Life/Energy always Creates according to my consciousness.

When the Abundant, Successful, and Loving Energy of God flows through my being, and my being is clouded with ideas of disappointment, resentment, and underachievement, God/Life/Energy, because of its nature, Creates corresponding experiences in my life. Similarly, when that same Abundant, Successful, and Loving Energy of God flows through my being, and my being is imbued with ideas of Perfection, Harmlessness, and Victory, God/Life/Energy, because of its nature, Creates corresponding experiences in my life of Perfection, Harmlessness, and Victory.

God is All That Is. God is the Fire in the Sun. This Fire of All Creation is only experienced inside my mind. The Sun appears to be outside of me, however my perception of the Sun takes place within the visions of my mind. This Radiant ball of fire resides in the heart of my mind and being. Shining brilliantly, this ball of fire is the spark of Creation residing within me. God is within me radiating Abundance, Success, and Love ceaselessly.

God is always in all ways expressing the reality of God through me at the current level I believe and accept. With God working through me, all my thoughts, feelings, and words are acted upon by God the instant I Create them. I therefore wisely Choose the things I decide to Create in my life experience. I Accept and Know that God is being the things I Choose to Claim and Believe in. I release all doubts and anxieties about my Creations, which God supplies for me with Certainty in the right way at the right time.

There are no unrealistic Dreams within the mind of God. There are only unrealistic time lines within the mind of man. With God working through me, my Success is a Certainty. My Dreams and desires are the forces that shape my reality. God Gives Ongoing Direction within my experience through my Dreams. When I honour my Dreams and follow the guidance I receive from God, I continually move to new experiences, which further the growth of my Dreams. When I follow my Dreams, I feel Joy. Through my experience of God's Joy, I AM Abundantly rewarded.

God is All. Since God is All, God is All I could ever Dream about in my experience. God is everything I Claim and Believe with all my heart, mind, and being. I Claim and Believe with all my heart, mind, and being that I AM One within God, and that God is All within me. My contemplation of Love, Life, and God Creates my experience of Love, Life, and God.

God is everything I could ever Dream about. God is my perfect connection to God's Love in the Universe I claim and believe in. I Love my clear and open communication with God in the form of my prayers being manifested and in the form of my clear and unmistakable advice received from God. I Love connecting with God daily through purification activities, through my constant sense of inner peace with God, and through my magical experiences of spirit with God. I Love resonating with Love and releasing all my past pains, present problems, and my future fears. I Love my spontaneous experiences through God. I Love pausing and immediately receiving clear signs from God as to the current steps in my life that Create miracles, which further develop my connection to God's Love. I Love that all my experiences nourish and nurture me deeply Now.

God is the Fiery Sun which seems to be in the sky in physical experience, but which is only perceived within me. This Fiery Sun sometimes seems to be clouded over, however this is the great illusion of physical experience. God the Sun and Spiritual Guiding Father is constantly shining and shining within me. In my past, I have Chosen to Believe in the illusion of physical experience. Now I Choose to Claim and Believe only the Truth of God. God is always in all ways the Energetic Fire behind the illusions of physical experience.

I AM the Mind within God Choosing what I Claim and Believe in. I Choose to view Only God in all my experiences. I Choose to view Only God's Abundance in all my experiences. I Choose to view God as my Awareness, Oneness, Decisiveness, Gratefulness, and Wholeness in all my experiences. And most importantly, I Choose God as the Fiery power to purify my Being. The Choices of my past, which prevent me from experiencing the Glory of God in all my experiences are what I purify.

I always make the perfect Choices in the perfect way and at the perfect time in my experience. However, as my vision of life expands and encompasses new concepts, my current Creations may still be informed by past Choices. Even though, I AM currently Choosing Loving, Successful, and Abundant outcomes, they can be halted by my deepest heartfelt most secret beliefs. This experience is perfectly natural in my growth towards Spirit. I always make the perfect Choices in the perfect way and at the perfect time in my experience. To further encourage my Creative powers, I use the Fiery Power of God to purify my Beliefs, seen and unseen by me.

In meditation, I purify my Heart, Mind, and Being with the Fiery Power of God. I envision the light from the Fiery Sun in the sky forming a beam of light that enters the Crown Chakra on top of my head and I Claim and Believe the following as God's light cleanses each of my Chakras.

Crown Chakra

I Choose God to be my clear Connection with God the Spiritual Guiding Father. The Fiery Energy of God purifies all my physical, mental, and spiritual pathways to access God's ever-present voice Giving Ongoing Direction within me. God is All.

Third Eye Chakra

I Choose God to be my clear connection with my Higher Self and Spirit Guides. The Fiery Energy of God purifies my emotionally guided opinions and connects me with the knowledge and understanding of my individualized Spirit within God. God is my Dreams.

Throat Chakra

I Choose God to be my Harmonious Experience of God's Love. The Fiery Energy of God purifies me and manifests through me as my Unconditional Love in Spirit, my Harmlessness and my Helpfulness in my thoughts, feelings, words, and in my actions. God is my Harmony.

Heart Chakra

I Choose God to be my Devotion and Love of Only God always in all ways. The Fiery Energy of God purifies my thoughts of Love and Devotion whereby Only God is all I perceive and experience within and without me. God is my Unconditional Love.

Solar Plexus Chakra

I Choose God to be my Knowledge and Wisdom. The Fiery Energy of God purifies all my feelings. I AM Open and Spontaneous within God. I laugh, cry, and express my feelings as God through me when they arise. God is my Wisdom.

Navel Chakra

I Choose God to be my experience of Joy and Gratitude. The Fiery Energy of God purifies my emotions (my present feelings triggered by my past experiences). I Choose God's Joy within, rather than searching for happiness in my outer experiences. God is my Present Joy and Gratitude.

Root Chakra

I Choose God to be my experience of Health and Wealth. The Fiery Energy of God purifies my Life Power and Energy. My Belief in God's Energy manifests as my Health and Wealth. God is my Wholeness.

The Fire of God purifies my Creative pathways. I Choose to purify my Creative pathways within God, when I decide to Create new Dreams. Each moment I let go a little more. I let God Love me a little more. I let God Guide me a little more. I let God Provide for me a little more. With all my Chakras purified they radiate the vibrant colours of the rainbow in beautiful clockwise rotating Energy wheels of Love and Light. These colours combine together to Create the brilliant white light Aura of God's Love Surrounding, Protecting, and Providing for me Always in All Ways.

I AM FIRE

*I Claim and Believe with all my
Heart, Mind, and Being
that I AM One within God
and God is All within me.*

I AM EARTH

I AM Fire. The Light of God purifies my body, mind, and soul transforming my entire being into a temple available to house the Power of God and transfer the Love of God to others and myself. God is the Sun and Spiritual Guiding Father within me.

God is also the Earth and Physical Providing Mother within me. The Earth Mother appears to be around me, however this is the great illusion of physical experience. Earth the Physical Providing Mother is constantly Creating physicality and manifesting that physicality within me. The process of Creation occurs on an energetic level first. The Earth Mother is always in all ways the Energetic Garden of Eden behind the illusions of my physical experience.

I AM the Heart, Mind, and Being within God Choosing what I Claim and Believe in. I Choose to view Only God in all my experiences. God is the Sun and Spiritual Guiding Father. The Fire of God purifies my Creative pathways. God is also the Earth and Physical Providing Mother. The Earth of God provides The Creative Substances of Physicality. The Creative Substances of Physicality are always within my Heart, Mind, and Being.

Within me there is a beautiful Garden of Eden. This Garden is made up of everything I Believe in. Whether the things I believe divide or Provide the Creative power to my Dreams, they are always Created within my Garden of Eden by me. My inner Garden Creates my outer experiences.

From the vantage point of God, everything provides the key to my wholeness within God/Life/Energy perfectly. Everything invites me to Be Whole within God/Life/Energy. In my past, I Chose to Believe that my experiences were either good or bad, as I saw fit. Now, I Choose to Believe that all my experiences are Perfect, as God sees fit. These experiences and Beliefs are always Created and Supported within myself.

The Garden of Eden within me is a lush Garden. This Garden contains everything I could ever imagine, and everything I have yet to even imagine. Within my Garden of Eden there is a beautiful tree. This Tree represents God, Life, and Love. This Tree holds the Eternal Support and Abundance of God within its being. This Tree makes up my Heart, Mind, and Being.

The roots of my Tree reach far into the Earth Mother. The roots of my Tree are made up of all the thoughts, feelings, words, and actions of my life. Some are straight. Others are crooked. Some are weak. Others are powerful. Some reach far into the Earth Mother. Others barely enter the Earth Mother's surface. However, they all work together to support and supply my Tree with Creative matter. More accurately, they act as the pathway for the Energy of God to flow through me.

The trunk of my Tree is large and straight to support all the Energy of God flowing to my branches. The branches of my Tree are my many talents and abilities. My talents and abilities are supplied by the Energy of God in my life. The Leaves of my Tree are all of my Dreams manifested by God through me in my life.

My Tree within my Garden of Eden has gone through many seasons, cycles, and changes during my life. Now, I Consciously Choose to purify my Tree with the Fire of God. I use the Fiery Energy of God to clear any and all blockages within my entire being. I use the energy to burn away the roots (that I remember and the ones I have forgotten) which do not allow the Energy of God to powerfully flow through me. I Choose to purify the energy centres within my trunk. I consciously activate my Chakras to vivify and strengthen my trunk while clearing away the old belief systems that I have held onto, which have knotted and taken their toll on my being. I Choose to cut off my branches that are weak. I Choose to leave my strongest productive branches so they can spread out to receive the maximum light of the Sun. I Choose to Create my Tree to be towering, strong, and majestic within my internal Garden of Eden.

I AM the Heart, Mind, and Being of God Choosing what I Claim and Believe in. I Choose to see the brilliant light of the Sun within me. God is my Sun and my Spiritual Guiding Father. The Fire of God purifies all my Creative pathways. God is also my Earth and my Physical Providing Mother. The Earth of God provides all the Creative Substances of Physicality. The Mind of God allows me to Choose what I Claim and Believe in. I AM the

Mind in my experience Choosing to Accept Guidance through God the Spiritual Guiding Father, Giving Ongoing Direction. I AM the Mind in my experience Choosing the Substances of Physicality through Earth the Physical Mother. I AM the Mind in my experience Choosing to surrender my requirements to the Mind of God understanding that my expectations limit the Loving, Successful, and Abundant nature of God to a few paths instead of the infinite path ways available within the Mind of God.

In meditation, I open my Heart, Mind, and Being and Accept the Creative Substances of Physicality provided through God the Earth Mother.

Physical experience is a balance of energies: positive and negative, light and dark, Yin and Yang, masculine and feminine. These energies make up the Whole that is God/Life/Energy. These energies are One Energy. This One Energy Manifests as different degrees of God, just as hot and cold are only different degrees of temperature.

I purify my Heart, Mind, and Being with the Fire of God and open all my Chakras to the degrees of physical experience provided through the Earth Mother. For me, these degrees Manifest as polarities that take the forms of two snakes, one light and one dark. The snake is the symbol of healing and transmutation exemplified by the Birth-Death-Rebirth cycle of a snake shedding its skin. The skin represents old patterns and beliefs. In the process of shedding old patterns, the snake becomes vulnerable before fully Accepting new Habits. In my Garden of Eden the two snakes climb clockwise around the trunk of my Tree providing their healing energy to my Heart, Mind, and Being as I open up to my vulnerability.

Root Chakra

I Choose God to be my experience of physicality within the Earth Mother. The energy of the Earth Mother provides all the Creative Substances of Physicality to Support and Prosper my experience. God is All.

Navel Chakra

I Choose God to be my experience of Creative and Sexual expression. These joyous energies put me in direct contact with God's Creative power. These energies birth all my experiences. God is birth.

Solar Plexus Chakra

I Choose God to be my experience of Personal Power. With my emotions released, my feelings flow freely and empower me to Choose God's Joy always in all ways. God is my Joy and Gratitude.

Heart Chakra

I Choose God to be my experience of Love and Devotion. My Love and Devotion within God empowers others and myself. God is my Unconditional Love.

Throat Chakra

I Choose God to be my Personal Expression of God. All of my thoughts, feelings, words, and actions reflect the Love of God. God is my Harmony.

Third Eye Chakra

I Choose God to be my Visions of God. All of my Visions flow from the Will of God. These Visions release my emotionally guided opinions, whereby I Accept God Giving Ongoing Direction within me. God is my Dreams.

Crown Chakra

I Choose God to be my Spiritual Experience of God on Earth. Although I AM in physical form, I have many incredible experiences that affirm my spiritual nature. God is my Spirit.

The snakes represent the extreme opposite courses of action within The Body of God. In my past, I Chose to go to the extremes in my experience to feel alive through my idea of Love, Life, and God. Now, I Choose neutrality to Live as Love, Life, and God. God witnesses every experience without judgement, from a point of neutrality. When I Consciously Choose neutrality as my inner experience, I realize I can release the outer experiences which previously bit me along with the old skin of limiting beliefs that I used to protect me from my fullest experience of Love, Life, and God. I join these snakes around the Tree of Love, Life, and God within my Garden of Eden. These energies form my backbone of Peace, Harmony, Gentleness, and Neutrality within my experience. I AM Fire.

I AM EARTH

Like Water, I follow the path of least resistance, which invites me to new experiences.

These experiences encourage my Wholeness within the Oneness of God.

When I float effortlessly along with the current of the Universe, God always delivers me to better shores than I imagine.

I AM WATER

I AM Fire. I AM Earth. I consciously Choose to purify my entire being through the four elements of physicality. Fire purifies through spiritual flames that transform old and outmoded thoughts, feelings, words, and actions into crystal clear experiences of Love. When I see old experiences with new eyes of Only Love, I can accept the knowledge and wisdom into my being and release the emotions I previously Chose to hold onto. Earth provides the Creative matter to form my new Dreams on a mental and spiritual level within my internal Garden of Eden.

Water is the third element of physicality. Water is a part of almost everything in physical experience. Water is in the air I breathe, the food I eat, the fluids I drink, and it is the prime element in my physical body.

Water is the manifestation of emotions. Emotions are different from feelings. Feelings are a natural flow of God's Energy through me, in the moment, whereas emotions are my feelings informed by past experiences. Emotions communicate a need for cleansing. When my past emotions take precedence over my present feelings, my entire being becomes unbalanced. In my past, I have changed decisions I felt were appropriate because of the emotional baggage I chose to hold onto.

Whereas Fire burns hot and bright to purify, Water cleanses with a gentle and soothing nature. This is a slower process in many ways, however this process is very deep and very permanent. Water's slow and gentle process eventually wears down the greatest emotional mountains, which I constructed out of the molehills in my experience.

On one level, Water is an emotional barometer encouraging me to release my emotionally guided opinions. I utilise Water to soothe my aching body, which occurs when I am holding onto outmoded emotions. I utilise water to cry away my long held suffering. I utilise water to release all my thoughts, feelings, words, and actions that do not encourage my connection within God.

On another level, Water represents my mental and spiritual blueprint (my Dreams) of my Health and Wealth. Water is both the fountain of youth and the flow of Abundance within my inner Dreams.

Water both washes and nurtures the Garden of Eden within me. Water washes away my old thought forms that believe in anything other than God as my Health and Wealth. Water also nurtures my Connection with God and nurtures my inner space so that my beliefs and Dreams can take root in my Garden of Eden.

My Dreams are powerfully Created when I mirror waters example and Choose to follow the path of least resistance. The path of least resistance always invites me to a fuller experience of my Oneness within God. In my past, I have Chosen to fight for particular Dreams. Now I follow the path that invites me. When I follow the path that invites me, I discover more about my relationship with God, which increases my Oneness with God, increases my ability to recognize all of God's gifts, and increases God's ability to manifest the perfect forms for me to experience my Dreams. When I go with the flow rather than against it, the resulting forms are closer to my imagined forms than when I fight for them.

I Claim and Believe in the Abundance of Water in all things. I Validate my inner world as the Creative river through which the Water of God flows. Like Water, I follow the path of least resistance, which invites me to new experiences. These experiences encourage my Wholeness within the Oneness of God. When I float effortlessly along with the current of the Universe, God always delivers me to better shores than I imagine. In my past, I fought against the current as I worked towards the particular forms I imagined my Dreams should take. When I did I felt unsupported and near drowning. Now I begin with my Faith (Feelings Automatically Inside my Truthful Heart) Knowing and Trusting that God fulfils all my Dreams in the right way and at the right time in the perfect forms to match the feelings I desire and hold deeply within my Heart, Mind, and Being.

In meditation, I open my Heart, Mind, and Being and access Water's loving and gentle nature. I welcome Water from the Earth Mother to cleanse my being thoroughly through all of my Chakras. I envision myself walking into a crystal clear lake. Its surface mirrors the cloudy sky above. This dark sky is overflowing with moisture gathered from all over the Earth Mother. As I step into the warm stillness of the lake, the rain begins to fall and its soothing sound surrounds me in Loving comfort. The rain pours out and with it I release my tears. My tears are not lost in the rain. They unify with the Earth Mother and add to Her nurturing touch, which soothes everyone that comes in contact with Her Life Blood.

Crown Chakra

I Choose God to wash away all my self-created blockages to God. Through unifying with the water of the Earth Mother I AM a blood cell in Her being, consciously Choosing to soothe others and myself on my journey. God is my Unity.

Third Eye Chakra

I Choose God to wash away all my self-created beliefs in anything other than the limitless nature of God. The rain washes over my head and cleans my Third Eye of all mud allowing me to see God's Visions clearly. God is my Clarity.

Throat Chakra

I Choose God to wash away all of my words about anything other than the glory in all of God's Creations. I drink Water as a reminder that I always make the choice as to whether my words horrify or Glorify. God is my Harmlessness.

Heart Chakra

I Choose God to wash away all of my deeply held beliefs that claim anything other than the God's Unconditional Love and Support for me. The water on my chest radiates with the warmth from the love in my heart. God is my Loving Warmth.

Solar Plexus Chakra

I Choose God to wash away all my feelings that no longer support who and what I AM. The Water that surrounds me acts as a conductor, drawing all energy from my body that dissipates my wholeness within God. God is my security.

Navel Chakra

I Choose God to wash away all of my feelings that no longer support Only God's Love through my Creativity and Sexuality. I wash away my self-created dramas around those experiences that cover up my essential nature. God is my joyful expression of my Creativity and Sexuality.

Root Chakra

I Choose God to wash away all of my feelings that support anything other than miracles. I swim in the Water and I AM Supported by the miracle of Water's nature. God is my physicality.

Water encourages me to slow down and swim with Joy. Water Washes and Cleanses me Physically, Mentally, Emotionally, and Spiritually. In my past, I tried to catch every ship that sailed by me believing that it would be the only one. However, God reminds me that there are many ships and that I can relax and enjoy the Water of life. I can Choose to swim in the nurturing Water, drink of its nourishing liquid, and cry to release long held suffering to fully experience my Joy. When the time is right and all the pieces have come together, the clouds in the sky part and the Sun Creates a glorious rainbow through the rain drops majestically announcing the arrival of the ship of my Dreams. I AM Fire. I AM Earth.

I AM WATER

When the time is right and all the pieces have come
together, the clouds in the sky part
and the Sun Creates a glorious
rainbow through the rain drops
majestically announcing
the arrival of the ship
of my Dreams.

Air is the ultimate reminder of Freedom.

Freedom   expects   nothing.

Air   expects   nothing.

God expects nothing.

Freedom just is.

Air just is.

God just is.

Freedom.

I AM AIR

I AM Fire. I AM Earth. I AM Water. I AM composed of the breath of God. The fourth element of physicality is Air. The Air of God allows me to breathe in the Love of God, while breathing out everything I have Created that believes in anything other than Only God.

The four elements of physicality purify my body when I follow the example Air shares. Air encourages me to flow with the nature of physicality rather than against it. When I flow with the nature of physicality, I feel its presence, yet I consciously Choose the spiritual nature behind physicality as my reality. The spiritual nature of physicality forever encourages Oneness with God.

Air is a great reminder of my Oneness with God. Air is the ultimate reminder of freedom. Freedom expects nothing. Air expects nothing. God expects nothing. Freedom just is. Air just is. God just is. When I follow the example of Air, I release my emotionally guided opinions, my expectations, and my desired results, and these choices allow me to just be who and what I AM in the moment.

Air reminds me to Choose Love and Freedom in every moment of Now. Love and Freedom is the process of Choosing the experiences or actions which help me to expand into new avenues expressing who and what I AM. Love and Freedom open me up to experience and act out new joy. Love and Freedom help me to stay in a peaceful space during adversity. Love and Freedom send my Love to everyone everywhere. Love and Freedom allow me to reveal my Truth to everyone everywhere every time. Love and Freedom remind me to give and share all I have with everyone whom asks. Love and Freedom is in the room to heal the room. Love and Freedom allow me to make amends with others and myself. Love and Freedom say 'yes'.

In meditation, I consciously access the power of Air through my breath to invigorate my chakras. Focussing on one chakra at a time, I take a deep breath through my nose, I hold that breath for seven heartbeats while visualizing my chakras spinning fluidly in a clockwise motion, and then I release all my tension held in my body as I exhale through my mouth. This process of relaxation allows me to fully access the Present moment as I become one with the invisible nature of God. As with all of my meditation practices, this process works wonderfully when I can access it in an uninterrupted outer space. However, through practice I AM able to Create that uninterrupted space within me, no matter what is taking place outside of me. During each breath, I visualize the light of the Universe entering my chakras and then my light returning to the Universe. In my past, I imagined that positive energy cleaned my space with each inspiration, while negative energy was released with each expiration. Now I realize that this energy is only inspirational. God inspires me to be the Grandest Feeling of God in every moment, and I inspire God to experience another part of that being. During this entire experience, I visualize the pure colours of the rainbow in my mind.

Crown Chakra

I Choose God to be my Love and Freedom. I envision the Air of God in the form of wind blowing through my violet chakra, increasing the flow and removing all tension and blockages. God is my Breath.

Third Eye Chakra

I Choose God to be my Clarity of Visualisation. The Air of God clears my mind of miscellaneous thoughts, increasing the flow of my indigo chakra. God is my spiritual sight.

Throat Chakra

I Choose God to be my Voice. My words Create vibrations in the Air of God. Through my blue chakra, air waves transmit my speech to those around me. God is my words of Peace.

Heart Chakra

I Choose God to be my heartbeat. My heartbeat moves oxygen through my body and loving energy to my entire being from my vibrant green heart chakra. God is my heartbeat of patience.

Solar Plexus Chakra

I Choose God to be my feeling nature. My yellow solar plexus chakra imagines my feelings as Only God's Love. God is my Feelings

Navel Chakra

I Choose God to be my Creative centre. I breathe my Creativity and Sexuality through my orange chakra. God is my Creative Breath.

Root Chakra

I Choose God to be my breath. With each red chakra breath I take I consciously remind myself of God's being. God is my Being.

Each breath of Air inhaled, held, and exhaled expands my experience of God's Breath. I consciously Choose to utilise God's Breath to remove all blockages to my wholeness with God. I AM Fire. I AM Earth. I AM Water.

I AM AIR

In my experience of physicality,
I cannot Create Transformation
in my outer experience

but

I can Create
the space for transformation to
occur in my inner experience ~ a space for
Love, Life, and God to enter my
Heart, Mind, and Being
transforming my
entire being

into

God's Manifestations.

I AM TRANSFORMATION

I AM Fire. I AM Earth. I AM Water. I AM Air. When the four elements of physicality come together they can Create a peaceful paradise or a strong storm. Both are the results of the systematic combination of the physical elements Fire, Earth, Water, and Air. Both are the results of the systematic combination of my Creatively powerful thoughts, feelings, words, and actions.

A strong storm is the result of the physical elements Transforming extreme energy use back to moderate energy use. During a storm, Fire manifests as lighting. The positive and negative charged particles of the Water Clouds and the Earth Mother share Fire's energy to balance each other out. A deluge of Water cleanses the Earth Mother of debris and renews her Water levels. Wind powerfully refreshes the dank Air of the Land. A storm very often is drastic and dramatic.

A peaceful paradise seems a more appropriate place to be, but many times represents a place of little or no movement in life. The process of Transformation can be one that I Choose to Create or one that I react against. In my past, I reacted against the opportunities presented to me through storm's energy. Since storm's energy uprooted my creations in my past, I perceived that energy as destructive instead of realizing that storm transformed the creations that no longer served my growth. The resulting new ground was perfect for Unifying growth and Wholeness within God to take root.

In my experience of physicality, I cannot Create Transformation in my outer experience, but I can Create the space for transformation to occur in my inner experience - a space for Love, Life, and God to enter my Heart, Mind, and Being and transform my entire being into God's manifestations. Now when a storm floods my experience, I open my being to its cleansing powers. I accept that this experience is powerfully preparing the way for my Dreams to manifest. In my past, the strongest of storms has been physical illness. The experience of illness totally knocked the Wind out of me in preparation for new growth.

I Create transformations through two main actions in my

life. The first action occurs by opening my Heart, Mind, and Being and accepting everything in my life that I find unacceptable. The second action is to push past my previous limitations of understanding and acceptability.

Whenever I find something unacceptable it generally means that I have not accepted it as a part of me, or more importantly as a part of God. I therefore Choose to Accept everything I find unacceptable. I Choose to Love what I previously judged as unlovable. I Choose to Forgive what I previously judged as unforgivable.

I Choose to Accept, Bless, and Love every experience as being a part of God. There is no such thing as good or bad. There is only my perception of what works and what doesn't work in Creating my Dreams. I Accept, Bless, and Love that every experience allows me another opportunity to unify with an aspect of God. When something tragic (like Death, Deceit, Divorce) happens in my experience, I Accept that it is a part of my experience allowing me an opportunity to Choose my highest Choice to Unify with All That Is God. I Bless the experiences, which allow me to Choose my highest Choice Supporting Unity with All That Is, and I Love that they allow me to Choose my highest Choice to Unify with All That Is - God/Life/Energy.

My Lowest Choice promotes separation from God through Fear, Judgement, and Rejection of anything and everything. My highest Choice Creating Oneness with All That Is, Accepts, Blesses, and Loves anything and everything in my experience.

Accepting, Blessing, and Loving anything and everything helps me push past my previous limitations. Each day opportunities suggest that I can push past my previous limitations. The voice of God, Giving Ongoing Direction within me constantly suggests things that I can be, do, or have next. Everyday I follow the voice that says, usually quietly, that I can be, do, or have new experiences just for the fun of them and I push past my previous limitations and try new things.

In everyday life, pushing past my previous limitations usually means stepping out of my comfort zone. I may be comfortable when I am living in a peaceful paradise. However, I experience little or no growth in Creating the life of my Dreams. Therefore, everyday I Choose to follow the voice that says I can be, do, or have a new experience, particularly when it is out of my comfort zone.

I know an experience is out of my comfort zone when the voice of my ego screams that I MUST NOT make a particular choice because of everything I stand to lose or gain in the process.

The voice of God, Giving Ongoing Direction says that I can make a Choice just for the experience of it, rather than for what I may gain or lose.

I can Choose to live a comfortable life in a peaceful paradise with its unexpected and strong storms that force me to open my heart instantly. I can also Choose to live a life that goes past my peaceful paradise by Creating expected and small storms within myself, whereby I open my heart to the limitless possibilities of God's Love within my Dreams.

In meditation, I transform my Heart, Mind, and Being into pure light by claiming every part of my experience as a part of me. I Accept, Bless, and Love everything and anything I have previously kept separate in my experience. I invoke all the elements of physicality to form a controlled storm within my being. This storm utilises the elements of physicality through my chakras to purify with Fire, cleanse with Water, and blow away with Air all energy that I have Created and held onto which restricts me from fully expressing who and what I AM in limitless ways in Earth's fertile physicality.

Crown Chakra

I Choose God to be my experience of Realisation. With God, I Realise all that had previously been unrealised within God. God is my Realisation.

Third Eye Chakra

I Choose God to be my experience of Acceptance. With God, I Accept all that I had previously found unacceptable within God. God is my Acceptance.

Throat Chakra

I Choose God to be my experience of Blessing. With God, I use my words to Bless everything that I previously rejected within God. God is my Blessing.

Heart Chakra

I Choose God to be my experience of Love. With God, I Love everything that I previously found unlovable within God. God is my Love.

Solar Plexus Chakra

I Choose God to be my experience of Forgiveness. With God, I Forgive everything that I previously found unforgivable within God. God is my Forgiveness.

Navel Chakra

I Choose God to be my experience of Surrender. With God, I Surrender to the flow within God instead of fighting against the flow. God is my Surrender.

Root Chakra

I Choose God to be my experience of Wholeness. With God, I Unite everything I previously found separate within God. God is my Wholeness.

When I consciously Choose to transform my entire being through the power of storm, I Unify the disparate aspects of my being into the Wholeness of All That Is. Now, my purified, birthed, cleansed, and breathing being of physicality constructs my Dreams on a spiritual level. Through my harmonised physical, mental, emotional, and spiritual being the energy of God powerfully transforms the elements of physicality into the forms that most effectively mirror the feelings I AM Creating within my being. I AM Fire. I AM Earth. I AM Water. I AM Air.

I AM TRANSFORMATION

My Highest Choice Creating Oneness with God
Accepts, Blesses, and Loves
everything.

My Clarity proposes that I AM the instrument
through which I can Choose God to Choose
the Grandest forms imaginable
to Create my Dreams.

I AM CLARITY

I AM Fire. I AM Earth. I AM Water. I AM Air. I AM Transformation. With Loving Gratitude working through me, I Release my attachments to my past emotions and my future expectations. My past emotions and my future expectations are self-Created limitations that I previously Chose to believe in. When I Choose them, these beliefs limit the ways in which the Feeling of God's Energy can manifest through me Right Here Right Now.

God is Unconditional Love. God's Energy is naturally Abundant, Successful, and Loving. God's Energy is constant. God's Energy is impersonal. It comes to every Heart, Mind, and Being in experience in the exact same Abundant, Successful, and Loving form. The only thing that is different for each Heart, Mind, and Being in experience is their individual thoughts, feelings, words, and actions.

God manifests whatever I Choose. In my past, I Chose to hold onto past emotions and future expectations. The Abundant, Successful, and Loving Energy of God flowed through my Heart, Mind, and Being, however God's Energy could only continue to Create and experience my past emotions and future expectations through me. As a result, I experienced memories and visions, rather than physical manifestations in the present. God can only Manifest through me what I Choose to Manifest within myself.

Clarity in my life results with my Awareness that God is All. I Claim and Believe with all my heart, mind, and being that God is All there is in experience. Through this truth, I AM One within God, and God is All within me. There is no separation. There is Only Oneness. Oneness with God. Oneness with All. I AM All. I AM God.

Clarity in my life results when I remember that God does not need or want anything. God is everything. God is the Source of everything. Since I AM One within God, I AM one channel through which God/Life/Energy manifests in life. As my channel, I AM the Source of that which I Dream about. I AM Creating my own Dreams. I AM the Source with God. As the source I do no need or want anything - I AM Everything.

I Choose to manifest my Dreams through any belief or belief system I Choose. I can believe in hard work, the power of my word, or any other thing I Choose to Believe in. In my past, I experienced some of my Dreams through these particular beliefs, but the Dreams that resulted usually did not Create the feelings I Imagined they would, or they lasted for an amount of time that was generally short. My Physical life is finite. My Spiritual life is Infinite.

Now, I Choose God to manifest through me what I Choose to manifest through myself. I Choose to manifest God in All my thoughts, feelings, words, and actions. God can take many forms. I can imagine a lot of forms. However, when I Choose God to Imagine through me, God can Imagine the Perfect forms always in all ways.

My Clarity allows me to Choose from limitless options. My Clarity reminds me to Choose any and everything in experience with the utmost Clarity. My Clarity encourages me to Choose what I AM Creating in the grandest forms imaginable. My Clarity proposes that I AM the instrument through which I can Choose God to Choose the Grandest forms Imaginable to Create my Dreams.

In my past, my ego (emotionally guided opinions) screamed against this form of openness with God. My ego stated that I would be giving away my ability to Choose my own Dreams. Where was the free will in that choice? My ego railed against any and every attempt I made to allow God to utilise me as an instrument of God. For years, I believed my ego.

Then, one day, I decided to Choose God to utilise me as an instrument of God. In no way did I consider myself to be a perfect instrument through which God could work, however God reminded me that my personal worth increased to myself and others every time I Choose to let God work through me.

This is a constant Choice. In my past, sometimes my Choices were affected with fear, and sometimes my Choices were affected with Love. Now, I AM Aware of my Choices and my Clarity has become ever present within my Heart, Mind, and Being. Now, I struggle less to make the highest Choice in situations. Now

I Choose God through me.

When I experience my Oneness with God as I write, or meditate, or pray, the highest Choice is a simple decision to access. When I experience my Oneness with God in other beings, the highest Choice is a simple decision. Whenever I experience my Oneness with God, my experience encourages me to make the highest Choice. It is only when I Choose to focus on anything other than my experience of my Oneness with God, reinforcing my beliefs in the possibility of separation from God (which is only possible within my mind), that the highest Choice becomes a difficult decision. No matter what choice I make, it is always my choice.

In the process of Creating my Dreams, the highest Choice always encourages me to Observe the Grandest Feeling of God. To desperately need or want a particular person, place, thing, or experience is never the Grandest Feeling of God. The Grandest Feeling of God reminds me that I AM One with God always and I HAVE the perfect people, place, things, and experiences right now to experience the Grandest Feeling of God definitely Right Now.

Therefore, Clarity in Creating my Dreams, does not desperately need or want. To need or want a thing in my experience makes it Clear to God that I do not have a particular experience, and to believe that I am separate from God results in God only being able to manifest through me what I Choose to manifest through myself.

God is All. I AM One within God. God is All within me. I AM the Source of my Creations. I Choose God to manifest God through me. I Choose the feelings I prefer to be in my experience. I choose to be Peace, Love, Joy, and Harmony. Through my chosen feelings I experience Clarity in my Awareness of the Grandest Feeling of God. My Clarity and Awareness of God Creates my Clarity and Awareness of my Dreams. I AM Creating my own Dreams means I AM Creating Clarity in my Awareness that my own Dreams are within God when I align with them Right Here and Right Now. God is all Dreams. I AM One Dream within God. God is all Dreams within me.

God, Love, and Life are interchangeable words to describe

All That Is in experience. God, Life, and Love give All to everything in experience and require nothing else to experience God, Life, and Love in every moment. I can also Give God, Life, and Love to All in experience and require nothing else to experience God, Life, and Love in every moment. For what I give to life, I live. I Give Joy, I live Joy. I Give Blessings, I live Blessings. I Give Dreams, I live Dreams.

I AM the Source. Whatever I desire to experience, I can Give to All in experience and require nothing else to experience that All. When I desire to experience my Dreams, I can Give my Dreams to All in experience and require nothing else to experience my Dreams. I can Give my Love to All in experience and require nothing else to experience my Love. I can Give my Happiness to All in experience and require nothing else to experience my Happiness. I can Give my Abundance to All in experience and require nothing else to experience my Abundance.

Many times in my past, I tried to Receive All in experience, but found I required All things to experience any thing. I tried to receive my Love from All in experience, but found I required All Love to experience any Love. I tried to receive my Happiness from All in experience, but found I required All Happiness to experience any Happiness. I tried to receive my Abundance from All in experience, but found I required All Abundance to experience any Abundance.

It empowers me to Give when I Give to Live my life to the fullest as the Grandest Feeling of God just for the experience of it. I Choose to Give to myself when it allows me to Live the Grandest Feeling of God expressed through me. I Choose to Give to others when it allows me to Live my Grandest Feeling of God expressed through me. I Give my time to others to Live my Grandest Feeling of God expressed through my use of Time. I Give Money to others to Live the Grandest Feeling of God expressed through my use of Money. I Give because it brings me Joy, not because I should or I have to. I Give to Live my life to the fullest as the Grandest Feeling of God just for the experience of it.

It empowers me to Receive when I Receive to Live life to the fullest as the Grandest Feeling of God just for the experience of it. I Choose to Receive what I AM offered when it allows me to Live the Grandest Feeling of God expressed through me. I Choose to Receive Abundance, Joy, Love, and Happiness from everyone including myself when it allows me to Live my life to the fullest as the Grandest Feeling of God just for the experience of it. I Choose to Receive because it brings me Joy, not because I should or I have to. I Receive to Live my life to the fullest as the Grandest Feeling of God just for the experience of it.

Through my Awareness and Clarity I Choose to recognise my truth that God is on my side. Through my Awareness and Clarity, I Choose to recognise my truth that God is inside me. Through my Awareness and Clarity I AM Creating my own Dreams by recognising that my Dreams are already manifested within God. I AM Fire. I AM Earth. I AM Water. I AM Air. I AM Transformation.

I AM CLARITY

My Dreams are formed by
my Intentions mixed with my Clarity
which Remind me that

God is on my Side,
Everything is Perfect,
and
There is nothing to worry about.

I AM INTENTION

I AM Fire. I AM Earth. I AM Water. I AM Air. I AM Transformation. I AM Clarity. My Awareness of the nature of God makes it Clear that God is absolutely everything in experience. There is nothing that is not God. This means that my thoughts are God/Life/Energy as well.

Since my thoughts are God/Life/Energy they have the power to Create. In fact all my thoughts, feelings, words, and actions are God and they all have the power to Create. My Clarity of thoughts, feelings, words, and actions are very important when Intending my Dreams.

I can allow my energy to move Consciously or unconsciously within my being. I can Choose to follow my thoughts wherever they lead me or I can Choose to lead my thoughts wherever I AM going. But until I AM Aware that there is a difference, I follow more often than lead.

In my past, my deeply held beliefs Created my experience for me unconsciously. Somewhere in my past, I had made a Conscious decision to believe something. Once that decision had been made, I Choose to never think about it again. As a result my once Conscious decision began to inform my experience without Consciously paying attention to any new information. When I did this, I began running on unconscious pilot.

A simple example of unconscious pilot working in my life occurs when I Chose to Give to others. In my past, I believed that I Consciously Chose to Give to others to Live my Grandest Feeling of God through me. In that moment of choice, I chose that. However, after a while, I found that more people requested the things I had to Give, I found that I resented Giving to all of them, or I found that Giving became a chore I felt I had to do rather than a Choice I made in the moment. I had begun to run on unconscious pilot. Now I Choose in every moment to Live the Grandest Feeling of God through me. Sometimes I Choose to Give to others. Sometimes I Choose to not Give to others. It is always my Choice. I Choose to make it Consciously in each moment. I AM a Conscious Pilot.

Being A Conscious Pilot means I AM always Choosing. I always have a choice. It is my Intention to be a Conscious Pilot always in all ways. To get to this place of being A Conscious Pilot I first become Aware of there being such a thing. I become Aware of this possibility through reading books, like this one, and through sharing with people I meet whom are on a similar journey. Once I become Aware of the possibility, I discover more books that talk about it and I meet more people that speak about it. These ideas Create a greater sense of Clarity within myself which fosters a belief in the greatest reality of God as the Source and Supply of everything in my experience.

With Clarity in my belief, I begin to experience these new possibilities for myself. More accurately, I begin to recognise that I experience these realities all along. My Clarity in belief Creates my Clarity in experience. Where before, I had been an unconscious pilot and Chose to blindly follow past Choices. Now I Choose to be A Conscious Pilot and recognise all my Choices, past and present in every moment of Now.

With Clarity in my Awareness and my Experience, I Choose to be a Conscious Pilot Constantly through my Awareness and my Experience. This Clarity reminds me that my Dreams are formed by my Intention mixed with my Clarity, which inform me that God is on my side, everything is perfect, and there is nothing to worry about.

Through my Intention I AM Self-Empowered. Self-Empowerment for me means that I Choose and Declare who and what I AM without the need for any approval from outside myself. I look only to The Feeling of God within me as my Source and Supply, and I do not need any approval in that process. I AM Self-Empowerment by being Oneness in my Awareness with whatever I wish to experience through my Oneness with God.

God is everything in experience. My Contemplation of God as my world experience Creates my world experience. I contemplate my being in Oneness within the Being of God, which Creates my recognition of the Perfect people, places, and things in my experience. Whatever I Choose to experience is already a part of the Being of God. I AM One within God as well. My Intention is to fully Align with, Allow, and Accept that God, my Dreams, and I are One. When I Choose to experience more of anything in my life, I do so by Choosing to remember that God is All in experience.

God is All. I AM One within God. God is All within me. God as my experience of Abundance becomes my life. God's Abundance is infinite. God's Abundance is over flowing. God's Abundance forever radiates in my world. Since God's Abundance is Only Love, Only Life, Only Oneness in my experience, God is everything there is to be through Abundance. However, God's experience of Abundance only occurs when I AM Abundance in my experience. It is through my Clarity and Intention of God's Abundance as Absolute that manifestation takes place. The Feeling of God within me only experiences Abundance through my manifestation of Abundance. God's Abundance comes to me from absolutely everywhere in experience. God's Abundance comes to me in the Perfect people, places, and things every day in every way. When I AM One with God's Abundance in my inner world, God's Abundance is manifested in my outer world.

Through my contemplation of this Truth of God, the Energy of God manifests in the physical world as the Perfect Job, Relationship, or whatever forms of Abundance I Choose to experience. Whatever I Choose to experience, I contemplate God's Perfection working in my life to provide the Perfect people, places, and things as that experience. I Choose the Dreams I prefer to experience and then I Observe God's Oneness with my Dreams within me. I AM Fire. I AM Earth. I AM Water. I AM Air. I AM Transformation. I AM Clarity.

I AM INTENTION

My Intention is to fully Align with, Allow, and Accept that God, my Dreams, and I are One.

I AM CERTAINTY

I AM Fire. I AM Earth. I AM Water. I AM Air. I AM Transformation. I AM Clarity. I AM Intention. God is All. I AM One within God. God is All within me. This Certainty informs my entire experience. God is the Source and Supply of all my Dreams. God is All Dreams. I AM One Dream within God. God is All Dreams within me.

My Dreams are the suggestions of God, Giving Ongoing Direction in my life. God's Voice within me continually suggests new things that I Can be, do, or have. This Voice reminds me that I Can be, do, or have new Dreams just for the experience of them. There is rarely pressure associated with the voice of God, Giving Ongoing Direction.

My ego (emotionally guided opinions), however, usually screams to me that I MUST have particular people, places, and things in my experience because they allow me to win when I have them or lose when I do not. Whenever I find that the voice of my ego is screaming that I MUST be, do, or have something, I Choose to let go of my expectations and let God be my Perfection.

I AM Certainty when I let God be my Perfection through Self-Reflection. Self-Reflection reminds me to look deep within for my Oneness with God. This Oneness is my Truth. This Oneness is my Centre. This Oneness is my Certainty. This Oneness is my core belief. I AM Creating My Own Dreams of Oneness with God. This is my experience of total Unity with All in experience including my Dreams.

In human form, there is so very much to experience through physicality. In human form, there is so very much to experience through God's Presence. The Feeling of God within me is there for me to experience entirely. The more I contemplate The Feeling of God within the Oneness of my being, the more The Feeling of God manifests through the Oneness of my being. When I contemplate the Love of God, I imbue my being with the Love of God and imbue my experience with the Love of God.

I know with Certainty that my Perfect Dreams come to fruition through my Oneness with God. God is All within me. My

Dreams are a result of God Giving Ongoing Direction within my being. God is the voice within me that continually suggests new Dreams that I Can be, do, or have just for the experience of them. I Choose to recognise that all my Dreams are a Certainty through my Oneness with The Feeling of God within me.

My Clarity tells me that God is All, I AM One within God, and that God is All within me. This Clarity reminds me that I Choose God as the Source and Supply of the things I wish to experience. I make the Choice. My Choice identifies God as the Source and Supply of my Dreams. My Clarity reminds me that I AM the only one who can Choose the things I desire to experience.

I AM the Heart, Mind, and Being of God within my personal experience. I AM the Heart, Mind, and Being of God who selects my Creations Always in All Ways. I Choose my Creations through the Creative powers of my thoughts, feelings, words, and actions. It is my thoughts, feelings, words, and actions that form the basis of my Intentions. My Intentions are my beliefs at the core level. My Intentions are the pathway through which God Manifests my Dreams.

Through my Intentions, I Choose what I Accept, Believe, and Have in my experience. My Intentions can run on unconscious pilot if that is my Choice, or they can run on Conscious Pilot when I Choose them to. Conscious Pilot occurs when I Choose to Be The Feeling of God through all my thoughts, feelings, words, and actions in the Present Moment.

Choosing to Be The Feeling of God occurs without trying. The Feeling of God is a state of Being. The Feeling of God does not occur in a state of trying, thinking, talking, or acting. Being is Being. Either I AM Being The Feeling of God, or I AM trying, thinking, talking, or acting The Feeling of God.

Trying to Be The Feeling of God, thinking about Being The Feeling of God, talking about Being The Feeling of God, or acting as if I AM The Feeling of God are all forms of Make Believe. When my Intentions are the forms of Make Believe, The Feeling of God coming through me can only form Make Believe - Illusions. However when my Intentions are imbued with Being The Feeling of God, The Feeling of God flowing through me Manifests as The Feeling of God.

When I AM Being The Feeling of God, The Feeling of God Creates through me. In my past, I utilised the process of Make Believe to Create Belief within my experience. Before I developed a deep sense of Belief, the Creation Process in my life was primarily an exercise in trying to Create particular people, places, and things, instead of an experience of Being with the Perfect People, Places, and Things. It is easy to get caught up in Make Believe. The voice of my ego screams that I Must be, do, or have particular experiences to be an expression of The Feeling of God. This focus continues to reinforce the power of ego in my life.

My Clarity reminds me that God is All Dreams within me, and that I Choose the Dreams I AM going to experience. Through my Intentions, I Choose what I Accept, Believe, and Have. Operating on Conscious Pilot, I Accept, Believe, and Have The Feeling of God as my Source and Supply. I AM Being The Feeling of God. This is my Certainty. I AM Oneness with my Dreams.

Through my Certainty, I Love who and what I AM. Who and what I AM is reflected by my particular Dreams. These Dreams are who and what I AM. I AM an individuation of God. My Dreams are God's Dreams. I Love my individual Dreams. I Love who and what I AM.

My Contemplation of God as my world Creates my world experience of God as my world. To Create my Dreams I Contemplate God in my Heart, Mind, and Being, which Perfectly manifests in my outer world in the right way and at the right time. To Create Dreams that are not physically in my outer world yet, I Create my inner world with Certainty and Clarity. When I can feel in my heart (Certainty) what I see in my mind (Clarity), I Align with, Allow, and Accept God/Life/Energy in my (inner) world, which forms my (outer) world. What I believe fully, I see fully.

I Visualise my particular Dreams with Love and I Choose them with all my thoughts, feelings, words, and actions. I know that my Dreams are a Certainty within God. I Choose my particular Dreams, but I realise that I do not require them to be Whole and Complete within God. Always in all ways I AM Whole and Complete within God. With Loving Certainty My FAITH (Feelings

Automatically Inside my Truthful Heart) Create a space of Being The Feeling of God through me. This space Creates my Certainty of God's Loving support and my Dreams. I AM Fire. I AM Earth. I AM Water. I AM Air. I AM Transformation. I AM Clarity. I AM Intention.

I AM CERTAINTY

My Contemplation of God as my world Creates my world experience of God as my world.

Trying to Be The Feeling of God,
thinking about Being The Feeling of God,
talking about Being The Feeling of God,
or acting as if I AM The Feeling of God
are all forms of Make Believe.

When my Intentions are the forms of Make Believe,
The Feeling of God coming through me can only
form Make Believe - Illusions.

However when my Intentions are imbued with
Being The Feeling of God, The Feeling of God
flowing through me Creates The Feeling of God.

I AM FREEDOM

I AM Fire. I AM Earth. I AM Water. I AM Air. I AM Transformation. I AM Clarity. I AM Intention. I AM Certainty. For many years, I lived on unconscious pilot. My unconscious pilot followed my thoughts, feelings, words, and actions blindly. My thoughts, feelings, words, and actions were reacting against the people, places, and things of my experience. I spent my time analysing, judging, or worrying about the people, places, and things in my experience. At the extremes, I hated, feared, or attacked many people, places, or things in my experience because I followed my ego unconsciously.

Now I Choose to be a Conscious Pilot. I Choose The Feeling of God as my Only Source and Supply. I Consciously Choose to Transform my past rejection into present Acceptance and my future fear into present Love. In my past, I found myself hating, fearing, or attacking the people, places, and things in my outer experience, Now, I Accept with Unconditional Loving Certainty that The Feeling of God is my Only Source and Supply.

I Consciously Choose to Love, Bless, and Release my emotionally guided opinions (ego). I Consciously Choose to release my thoughts, feelings, words, and actions that focus on anything other than The Feeling of God as my Source and Supply. Through my Conscious Choice of Acceptance of The Feeling of God, I AM Freedom.

Freedom means that I AM Free from my expectations, so that I AM Free for God's Perfection. Through my Clarity, Intention, and Certainty, I know that The Feeling of God is my Source and Supply. God is All. I AM One within God. God is All within me. God is All my Dreams. God is All my thoughts, feelings, words, and actions that empower me to Be The Grandest Feeling of God. Anything that prevents me from Being The Grandest Feeling of God can be viewed as what does not work. Anything that presents me as Being The Grandest Feeling of God can be viewed as what works.

My ego demands that I continue to be my ego (emotionally guided opinions). However, my ego usually guides me to some form of restriction or limitation in my experience. My ego screams that I Must be, do, or have particular experiences because I win with them or lose without them. When I agree with my ego, I eventually suffer from my choice. That suffering can be as simple as doubtful thoughts or as difficult as hateful violence. No matter what level the suffering takes, it is suffering nonetheless.

The Feeling of God within me allows me to Be The Feeling of God. The Feeling of God suggests that I Can Be, Do, or Have new Dreams just for the experience of them. The Feeling of God suggests that I Can Surrender to the flow of life rather than resisting it. Surrendering to the flow of Life, Love, and God Creates Oneness with all of my experiences. When I resist the flow of Life, Love, and God in my experience, I separate my individual being from the flow of Life, Love, and God in my experience and this resistance denies all of God's Abundance in my experience.

When I resist God, my resistance persists. When I fight my life experience, I invite that life experience to continue. When I deny who and what I AM, I rely on who and what I am not.

When I surrender to God, I remember with God. When I Bless my perceived challenges, I Caress my challenged perception with Love. When I Observe my life experience with Love, I Love my life experience as they Deserve to Be.

Freedom allows me to care less about the forms and Live More of The Feeling of God. The forms are the illusions of life. God/Life/Energy is the Cause of Life. The forms are my life experiences. When I live in the forms, I become dependent on the success or failure of particular forms and I become caught up in the whims of each cycle of success and failure. My dependency on forms – Creates further dependency for my being. Whereas, my enjoyment of my present Feelings (whatever they may be) – Creates my further enjoyment of my present Feelings. I AM Freedom when I Surrender, Accept, and Honour every moment of Now as God's Greatest Gift to me.

Freedom reminds me that I can think less to Feel More. When I think about the forms of my experience, whether they are in the past, the present, or the future, they usually remind me of pain, problems, or challenges in my experience. My thoughts can also remind me of pleasures, but those past, present, or future pleasures many times turn into pain when they are not Created or reCreated in my present experience Now.

When I Feel More by opening my Heart, Mind, and Being to The Feeling of God as my experience, The Feeling of God results. The only moment of Creation is this moment Right Here Right Now. If I think about past pains, present problems, or future fears, I continue to Create those very experiences. Thinking about those things does not transform them. Thinking of past pains, present problems, or future fears only allows me to Be pain, to Be problems, and to Be fears. I do not desire to further Create those experiences, but whatever I think about I continue to Create. When it is said that way, it seems so obvious.

My inner world Creates my outer world. I AM Free to fill my inner world with whatever I Choose. In my past, I Chose to operate on unconscious pilot by blindly following whatever my thoughts, feelings, words, and actions reacted to.

Now, I Choose to Be a Conscious Pilot when I think less to Feel More. I Choose to Feel More of The Feeling of God within me. The Feeling of God is not found in my past memories, my present challenges, or my future expectations. The Feeling of God is not found in my knowledge, my beliefs, or my ideas. The Feeling of God is Only found in the Peace and Stillness within me.

To get in touch with The Feeling of God, I get in touch with whatever I AM Feeling right Now. What am I feeling right Now? Where am I feeling right Now? The Feeling of God within me is my Awareness or my Observation of The Feeling of God within my Inner World. Where is my Awareness of The Feeling of God? Is it in my head? Is it in my heart? Is it in my hands? Does it in manifest within my entire body? The reality of The Feeling of God (my I AM Presence) is that it is wherever I place my Awareness or my Observation onto that Presence within me.

When I think, the only things I get in touch with are my past memories, or my future expectations. But when I Feel I get in touch with The Feeling of God within me. Feeling is only about feeling. Feeling is not about my thoughts mixed with my feelings. Most often my emotionally guided opinions (ego) are my present thoughts mixed with very strong past feelings. When I AM Feeling, I release all my thoughts, perceptions, and judgements about my experience. Feeling releases my limitations.

So what am I feeling Right Now and where am I feeling Right Now? I Open to my present feelings. I Feel my present feelings fully. I Create a space within me to Observe my Present feelings. I just Observe my feelings. I do not judge my feelings, I just feel them. I do not think about my feelings, I just feel them. As I Observe what I AM Feeling, I Create a space for The Feeling of God (my I AM Presence) to enter my being. When my I AM Presence is activated by my Observation within me I can Accept What Is. The Feeling of God is the only thing active within me when I Choose it to be that way.

When I bring my Awareness to The Feeling of God within me. I activate my I AM Presence. When I activate my I AM Presence, I bring Being into form. When I bring Being into form my sense of self is derived from Being The Feeling of God, not from my personality. When I AM Being a personality, that personality has a whole list of needs. When I AM Being The Feeling of God, I AM Whole and Complete Right Here Right Now, and everything extra that comes to me is a bonus in my experience.

When I think less to Feel More, I feel all feelings inside me, Only when I Accept and Honour what is my actual inner experience in the Now can I open to the possible Transformation of my inner experience through The Feeling of God. When I Open to the possibility of Feeling anger, sadness, or depression within me, my Openness allows me to observe my life experience with Unconditional Love. My Unconditional Love Accepts and Honours my life experience as it deserves to Be. Right Now, on some level this life experience is what I wish for to enable myself to express my Greatest Freedom in the greatest forms and Feelings.

On unconscious pilot, I deny and fight my inner experiences. On Conscious Pilot, I Accept and Honour my inner experiences. Acceptance is Freedom; Freedom from past pains; Freedom from present problems; Freedom from future fears; Freedom for God's Perfection. When I AM Free, I Consciously Access The Feeling of God within me to Consciously Observe everything The Feeling of God is and is available within me. The Feeling of God is not the thinker, not the talker, and not the reactor. The Feeling of God is the Feeler, the Listener, and the Creator.

To stay in touch with The Feeling of God, I go about my daily activities by keeping some part of my Awareness on The Feeling of God (my I AM Presence) within me. I know that I AM Being The Feeling of God when I experience the Freedom of calm relaxation through whatever I experience. When I AM The Feeling of God, I get lost LESS in my thoughts, my feelings, my words, my actions, and the forms of my outer world. When I AM The Feeling of God, I experience past pains, present problems, or future fears, but I Freely and easily release them by placing my Awareness back onto The Feeling of God within me. When I AM The Feeling of God, I AM Whole and Complete wherein I no longer experience any need to be where I am not, to do what I have not done, or to have what has eluded me. When I AM The Feeling of God, I AM One with The Being within me. God is All within me.

Being The Feeling of God occurs when I AM Being the Joy underneath my pain, when I AM Being the Solution within my problems, when I AM Being the Love inside my fear, and when I AM Being the Unity Connecting my separation. Being The Feeling of God with my entire body reminds me to feel my inner world whenever possible – whatever feelings come up – until what comes up is Always in All Ways The Feeling of God manifested.

So I care less about my expectations, to Live More of God's Perfection. I blame less to Gain More. I think less to Feel More. I try less, to Be More. I talk less to Listen More. I react less to Create More. I judge less to Love More. I express less attitude and More Gratitude. I AM the Freedom of the Perfect feelings Here and Now not the particular forms there and then.

In my past, I cared more about my expectations, I thought more about my memories, I tried more of what I perceived would work, I talked more about what I thought people needed to do, and I reacted more to all my experiences. Now I know through my Clarity, Intention, Certainty, and Freedom that God is on my side, everything is perfect, and there is nothing to worry about when I contemplate The Feeling of God within my Heart, Mind, and

Being.

Every single moment of Now provides me with the Perfect opportunity to move one step closer to my Dreams, no matter what illusions may appear to be in my experience. This moment holds the key for this moment. This key has nothing to do with anything other than Being The Grandest Feeling of God in this very moment. This moment allows me the key opportunity to Choose to Be The Grandest Feeling of God – in whatever way I Choose to Be The Grandest Feeling of God. This moment does not hold the key to my future Dreams. This moment is the key opportunity to experience my Perfect Dreams Now. What Perfect Dreams of Being do I Choose Now? Is my Dream to Be Freedom Now? Is my Dream to Be Love Now? What is MY Dream in this moment here and now?

My present Dreams of Being are met in every moment of Now when I Choose to Be The Grandest Feeling of God in the Perfect way for me Now. This moment of Now is Perfect. My future Dreams of Being will be met in my future when I Choose to Be The Grandest Feeling of God in the Perfect way and at the Perfect Future time. There is nothing I can do about the future unless it is my present. The sooner I Choose the Dream opportunity in this present moment, the sooner I AM Free to Choose The Feeling of God to Be my Dreams. It is my Choice alone. No one else can make my choices for me.

A choice between the polarities of what works or what doesn't work is a choice for the same thing separated only by time. Happiness and unhappiness are two polarities of the same thing separated only by time. Abundance and lack of abundance are two polarities of the same thing separated only by time. When I focus on the forms of my experience like Happiness, Abundance, or Love in a relationship, I can Choose to let those forms make me happy when they provide me with what I imagine and unhappy when they do not. However, every time I Choose the forms in my outer world it works in exactly the same way. There is a cyclical nature of highs and lows inherent in the impermanence of forms.

The Permanence of The Feeling of God however, is never affected by the impermanence of forms. The Feeling of God only is Permanence. When my Contemplation is upon The Feeling of

God, the only impermanence available is my decision to Be The Feeling of God or not. As a Conscious Pilot, I Know that I Choose to experience the reality of The Feeling of God within me or not. As a Conscious Pilot, I Know that I Choose to experience my Faith (Feelings Automatically Inside my Truthful Heart) or my fear (Feelings Eroding Away Reality). As a Conscious Pilot, I Know that I Choose to Be The Heart, Mind, and Being of God or the heart, mind, and being of man. The Only Permanence in life is The Feeling of God.

Impermanence in life comes from my decision to not be The Feeling of God. Whenever I deny The Permanence of The Feeling of God, I rely on the impermanence of the forms of life. The impermanence of life experiences the cycles of good and bad, highs and lows, sickness and health, and the birth and death of physical forms.

The Only Permanence in life comes from my decision to Be The Feeling of God. The Permanence of The Feeling of God always experiences Being; never ending Being, never changing Being, never judging Being; never expecting Being; Always in All Ways. The Permanence of The Feeling of God Chooses for me what I Choose for myself; no expectations, no judgement, no changes; Only Being, Only Love, Only Life, Only God, Only Oneness. The Permanence of The Feeling of God reminds me to Choose what I AM Experiencing for myself Now, instead of fighting it, denying it, or resisting it. The Feeling of God reminds me to Choose my Dreams Now, Create my Dreams Now, and Live my Dreams Now with the Perfection that is in my experience right Now. I AM Free to Be The Feeling of God Always in All Ways. I AM Fire. I AM Earth. I AM Water. I AM Air. I AM Transformation. I AM Clarity. I AM Intention. I AM Certainty.

I AM FREEDOM

I AM The Presence Presents Present

I AM The Feeling of God (Presence)
within the Perfection (Presents)
in every moment of Now (Present)

I AM the Holy Trinity

I AM MANIFESTATION

I AM Fire. I AM Earth. I AM Water. I AM Air. I AM Transformation. I AM Clarity. I AM Intention. I AM Certainty. I AM Freedom. Everything other than The Feeling of God is impermanent and as a result experiences the cycles of good and bad, highs and lows, sickness and health, and the birth and the death of physical forms.

The Only Permanence in life is The Feeling of God. Through my Clarity of The Feeling of God in my life, I know that God is All, I AM One within God, and God is All within me. Through my Intention of The Feeling of God within me, I know that I Choose my Dreams as a Conscious Pilot and to Be The Feeling of God in every moment of Now I do not require any of my Dreams. Through my Certainty of The Feeling of God within me, I know that The Power of The Feeling of God expands within me each time I acknowledge, contemplate, and utilise The Feeling of God. Through my Certainty my Perfect Dreams are Whole and Complete within the Heart, Mind, and Being of God. Through my Freedom of The Feeling of God within me, I know that I AM Freedom from expectation and I AM Freedom for Perfection. These realisations come to me when I Accept The Feeling of God as the Only Permanence in my life.

By Choosing The Feeling of God first and only as the Permanence within my life, I Know that I do not need particular people, places, or things to experience a full and loving life. I experience a full and loving life by accessing The Feeling of God in every moment of Now. Right Now The Feeling of God as the Perfect people, places, and things are in my life allowing me to Create my Awareness within God, my Oneness within God, and my Dreams within God. Within this Perfection, I need nothing and I enjoy everything.

In my past, I had many expectations and I resisted the Perfection available to me in the Now. I followed the human creed - humans expect. I expected many things to be the way I envisioned and resisted everything that did not match my vision. I lived by the creed of conditional love and experienced a lot of pain in that process.

Unconditional Love only comes to fruition when I Choose to Accept everything as it is and open up to the Perfection in each moment of Now. I Choose to express The Feeling of God through me. The Feeling of God Accepts every person, place, and thing as Perfect. When I Accept everything as being the Perfect opportunity, my Manifestation experiences increase in my life.

When I embody Joy and Gratitude in my life, my Acceptance of the way life actually flows in my experience proceeds very quickly. I have discovered that my most powerful Manifestations come from Choices I make in the moment of Now by following The Feeling of God Giving Ongoing Direction within me. The Feeling of God suggests experiences that I can enjoy just for the enjoyment of them. My ego, on the other hand demands that I MUST be, do, or have particular experiences because I win with them or lose without them. When I AM Relaxed, I come from a calm and centred experience of Joy and Gratitude. From this place of Joy and Gratitude, it is easy to make a Choice that feels appropriate to my inner truth. When I AM Relaxed, my contemplation of The Feeling of God as my world experience Creates my world experience. When I AM Able to follow the voice of God Giving Ongoing Direction within me it becomes easier for me to Manifest God; Greatness Oneness Demonstrated.

In the Manifestation Experience, I combine my Clarity, Intention, Certainty, and Freedom with my Enthusiasm, Patience, Action, and Adventure.

I AM Enthusiasm through my Joy and Gratitude. I AM Joy by following the path that brings me the most Joy. I AM Grateful for the Perfect Opportunities that are in my experience in this and every moment of Now, which I Never Overlook Whatsoever. I express Gratitude every day in every way through my Joy and Acceptance of my Perfection.

I AM Patience by Being Mindful of my Direction and the Perfection in my life. My Patience comes by continually working with the Perfection that is in my life rather than what I imagine that Perfection could be. My Patience reminds me to Be Mindful of God's voice Giving Ongoing Direction. The voice of God communicates with me every day in every way. When Being Mindful of that Direction, I easily follow The Perfection. The Perfect Direction presents itself in the Perfect way and at the Perfect time. Through my Patience I always open to the Perfect opportunity when it presents itself.

I AM Action through my Transformation and my Manifestation. As life flows in its Perfection, I AM Reminded that I Can open my Heart, Mind, and Being to the Transformation of my perceptions of any past experiences when I Choose that Action. I AM Action by being Patience and then Opening to the Manifestation when the Perfect opportunities present themselves. I AM Action when I blame less to Gain More.

In my past, when I first became Aware of the power of my thoughts, feelings, words, and actions to Create my experience, it was easy to blame myself when my expectations were not met. When I blamed myself, I also chose to separate from The Feeling of God within me. Now I AM Aware of the power behind my thoughts, feelings, words, and actions whereby I blame less to Gain More. I Gain More when I Create Unity with The Feeling of God and Consciously Choose to see and to be the Perfection of God/Life/Energy Right Here Right Now.

I Choose to be God's Perfection by fully experiencing this moment whether it is full of perceived joy or perceived pain with the belief that opening my heart to my particular experience in this moment also opens my heart to create Unity with all the Abundance of The feeling of God.

I AM Adventure by going past my comfort zones. Whenever I find myself staying in a place where I feel comfortable, I AM also Choosing to stay in a place where I experience little or no growth. My Dreams are rarely experienced when I stay comfortable, whereas they are powerfully Manifested when I Choose to grow with the Perfect people, places, and things.

I AM The Feeling of God (Presence) within the Perfection (Presents) in every moment of Now (Present). I AM The Feeling of God's Now Perfection. I AM the Presence Presents Present. When I keep my Awareness of all three in Unity I flow easily within my life experience. When I remove my Awareness from one or more of these I Create separation. Unity in every moment of Now reminds me to open my Awareness to the Presence Presents Present. This Holy Trinity Manifests powerfully within my experience through me.

I AM Fire. God is the Sun and Spiritual Guiding Father within me Now. God is my Fire Now.

I AM Earth. God is the Earth and Physically Providing Mother within me Now. God is my Earth Now.

I AM Water. God is the Water and Mental Blueprint within me of my Health and Wealth Now. God is my Water Now.

I AM Air. God is the Air and my reminder of my Oneness within God Now. God is my Air Now.

I AM Transformation. God is the Storm and Unification of my Being Now. God is my Transformation Now.

I AM Clarity. God is All. I AM One within God. God is All within me Now. God is my Clarity Now.

I AM Intention. I Choose my Dreams, (without requiring them) and I AM The Feeling of God in the Now with the Perfection that is always available to me. God is my Intention.

I AM Certainty. I Choose The Feeling of God as my Source and Supply of my Perfection in the Now, which helps me realise my Dreams of Oneness with All. God is my Certainty Now.

I AM Freedom. I expect less and Perfect More in every moment of Now when I care less about my human personality and Live More of my God Presence. God is my Freedom Now.

I AM Manifestation. I AM Enthusiasm, I AM Patience, I AM Action, and I AM Adventure in every moment of Now when I AM The Feeling of God with All Perfection. God is my Manifestation Now.

I AM Creating My Own Dreams. I AM Presence Presents Present. The Only Permanence is The Feeling of God. The Only Moment is Now. Only my Presence Can know the Perfection.

Manifestation always occurs in the right way at the right time. The right way at the right time usually occurs when I AM ready to Surrender physically, mentally, emotionally, and spiritually to The Feeling of God for the support and growth of my Manifestations naturally.

In the name of and through the Power of The Feeling of God within me, I Allow the Perfect Manifestation of my Intention. My Intention is to Bless every Person on Earth through Manifesting my thoughts, feelings, words, and actions as The World's Greatest Unconditional Lover (Physical, Mental, Emotional, and Spiritual) as I Uplift and Encourage Joy and Potential within All That Is, as I Surrender all my limiting expectations, beliefs, desires, and judgements to experience the Overflowing Abundance and Blessings of God Now Here.

I AM Fire. I AM Earth. I AM Water. I AM Air. I AM Transformation. I AM Clarity. I AM Intention. I AM Certainty. I AM Freedom.

I AM MANIFESTATION

Ego screams that I MUST be, do, or have something because I win with it or lose without it.

God reminds me to Choose to be, do, or have something just for the experience of Love and Freedom and Joy in that choice.

I AM CREATING MY OWN DREAMS

There are no unrealistic Dreams in the Mind of God. There are only unrealistic time lines in the mind of man.

I AM Fire. I let go a little more. I let God Love me a little more. I let God Guide me a little more. I let God Provide for me a little more.

I AM Earth. I Claim and Believe with all my Heart, Mind, and Being that I AM One within God and God is all within me. In my past, I chose the extremes in my experience to feel alive through my idea of Love, Life, and God. Now, I choose Neutrality to Live as Love, Life, and God.

I AM Water. Like Water, I follow the path of least resistance that invites me to new experiences. These experiences encourage my Wholeness within the Oneness of God. When I float effortlessly along with the current of the Universe, God always delivers me to better shores that I imagine.

I AM Air. Air is the ultimate reminder of Freedom. Freedom expects nothing. Air expects nothing. God expects nothing. Freedom just is. Air just is. God just is. God is Love and Freedom. Love and Freedom open me up to experience and act out new joy. Love and Freedom help me to stay in a peaceful space during adversity. Love and Freedom send my Love to everyone everywhere. Love and Freedom allow me to reveal my Truth to everyone everywhere every time. Love and Freedom remind me to give and share all I have with everyone whom asks. Love and Freedom is in the room to heal the room. Love and Freedom allow me to make amends with others and myself. Love and Freedom say yes. Ego screams that I MUST be, do, or have something because I win with it or lose without it. God reminds me to Choose to be, do, or have something just for the experience of Love and Freedom and Joy in that choice.

I AM Transformation. I open to Transformation by accepting everything in my life that I find unacceptable. I cannot Create Transformation but I can Create the space within my inner experience - a space for Love, Life, and God to enter my Heart, Mind, and Being to transform my entire being into God's

Manifestation. My highest Choice Creates Oneness with God; Accepts, Blesses, and Loves everything.

I AM Clarity. My Clarity proposes that I AM the instrument through which I Choose God to Choose the Grandest forms imaginable to Create my Dreams. I give to live my life to the fullest as The Grandest Feeling of God just for the experience of that truth.

I AM Intention. My Dreams are formed by my Intentions mixed with my Clarity which remind me that God is on my side, Everything is Perfect, and there is nothing to worry about. God's Abundance is infinite. God's Abundance is over flowing. God's Abundance forever radiates in my world. Since God's Abundance is Only Love, Only Life, Only Oneness in my experience, God is everything there is to be through Abundance. However, God's experience of Abundance only occurs when I AM Abundance in my experience. My Intention is to fully Align with, Allow, and Accept that God, my Dreams, and I are One.

I AM Certainty. Trying to Be The Feeling of God, thinking about Being The Feeling of God, talking about Being The Feeling of God, or acting as if I AM The Feeling of God are all forms of Make Believe. When my Intentions are the forms of Make Believe, The Feeling of God coming through me can only form Make Believe - illusions. However when my Intentions are imbued with Being The Feeling of God, The Feeling of God flowing through me Creates The Feeling of God.

I AM Freedom. When I resist God, my resistance persists. When I fight my life experience, I invite that life experience to continue. When I deny who and what I AM, I rely on who and what I AM not. When I surrender to God, I remember with God. When I Bless my perceived challenges, I Caress my challenged perceptions with Love. When I Observe my life experience with Love, I Love my life experience as they Deserve to Be. This moment holds the key for this moment. This key has nothing to do with anything other than Being The Grandest Feeling of God in this very moment. This moment allows me the key opportunity to Choose to Be The Grandest Feeling of God – in whatever way I Choose to Be The Grandest Feeling of God. This moment does not hold the key to my future Dreams. This moment is the key opportunity to experience my Perfect Dreams Now. What Perfect Dreams of Being do I Choose Now? Is my Dream to Be Freedom Now? Is my Dream to Be Love Now? What is MY Dream in this moment here and now?

I AM Manifestation. I AM The Feeling of God (Presence) within the Perfection (Presents) in every moment of Now (Present). I AM The Feeling of God's Now Perfection. I AM the Presence Presents Present. When I keep my Awareness of all three in Unity I flow easily within my life experience. When I remove my Awareness from one or more of these I Create separation. Unity in every moment of Now reminds me to open my Awareness to the Presence Presents Present. This Holy Trinity Manifests powerfully within my experience through me. I AM The Presence Presents Present. I AM The Feeling of God (Presence) within the Perfection (Presents) in every moment of Now (Present). I AM the Holy Trinity

I AM CREATING MY OWN DREAMS

ABOUT THE AUTHOR

Barry Thomas Bechta is an artist, author, and film maker whose work centers around the concepts of Unconditional Love. Barry knew he wanted to write from a very young age and was encouraged with his artistic skills and only began writing full time in his thirties. He wrote his first book, *I AM Creating My Own Experience* as a personal journal to choose connection with God/Life/Energy. He has since written 17 inspirational spiritual books.

Barry loves to hear from people whom have connected with his writing and used it as a tool to improve their lives. If you would like to write him about your personal experiences as a result of reading any of his books, Barry encourages you to do so.

You can also get a Free Digital Copy of *I AM Creating My Own Experience - The Creation Vibration* from his main website:

www.unconditionallovebooks.com

Unconditional Love Books Titles of Related Interest
by Barry Thomas Bechta

I AM Creating My Own Experience
978-0-9813485-5-1

I AM Creating My Own Answers
978-0-9686835-1-4

I AM Creating My Own Dreams
978-0-9686835-2-1

I AM Creating My Own Relationships
978-0-9686835-3-8

I AM Creating My Own Abundance
978-0-9686835-4-5

I AM Creating My Own Success
978-0-9686835-5-2

I AM Creating My Own Happiness
978-0-9686835-6-9

I AM Creating My Own Experience - The Creation Vibration
978-0-9686835-7-6

I AM Creating My Own Experience - To Manifest Money
978-0-9686835-8-3

I AM Creating My Own Experience - 369 Conscious Days
978-0-9686835-9-0

Loving Oneness
978-0-9813485-0-6

Trust Life
978-0-9813485-1-3

I AM Creating My Own Financial Freedom - The Story
978-0-9813485-2-0

I AM Creating My Own Financial Freedom - The Lessons
978-0-9813485-3-7

Laughing Star's Guide to Laughter, Life, Love, and God
978-0-9813485-4-4

All of the above are books are available through your local
bookstore, or they may be ordered as digital downloads at
www.unconditionallovebooks.com

Barry Thomas Bechta is available for interviews, special events, workshops, and lectures that redefine, guide, and inspire everyone's connection to the Creative Power within themselves. To arrange author interviews, special events, workshops, or lectures, please contact:

**UNCONDITIONAL
LOVE BOOKS**

**Unconditional Love Books
Box # 610 - 2527 Pine St.,
Vancouver, BC, Canada V6J 3E8**

info@unconditionallovebooks.com

www.unconditionallovebooks.com

For additional copies of Barry's books, products, and services please contact your local book seller. Many products and services are Only available to order directly from the publisher as eProducts on the website.

Thanks for your purchase and Remember to Consciously Create your Life.

Right Now is the Only Moment of Creation

Enjoy it Fully!